AF255306

Something Special
Copyright © 2022 by Ryan Marsh

ISBN: 978-0-578-95722-7 (hardcover)
978-0-578-94549-1 (paperback)
978-0-578-95721-0 (ebook)
First Edition: April 2022

Something
Special

It was late afternoon and almost time for supper.

"Who's ready for a walk?" Dad asked.
"Do you think we'll see any animals?" Little Sister questioned.
"Yeah, I'll bet we will," declared Big Brother.
"Me too!" piped Big Sister.

As they left the house, they all hoped for something special.

A little ways from home, Big Sister shouted,
"Wow, what a pretty FLOWER!"
Dad smiled, "There's something special about a sunflower."
"Yeah, you can eat the seeds," announced Big Brother.

"That's true," Dad confirmed, "but there's more. The sunflower follows the sun as it moves across the sky. It's called *heliotropism*.

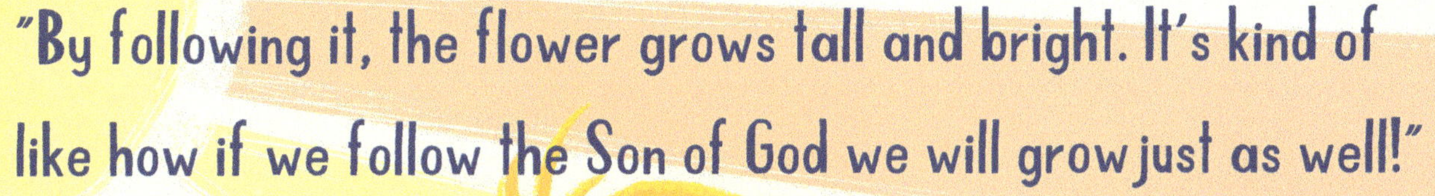

"By following it, the flower grows tall and bright. It's kind of like how if we follow the Son of God we will grow just as well!"

"Woah! Look at that CATERPILLAR!" Big Brother gasped.
"It's huge!"
Dad grinned, "There's something special about a caterpillar."

"I know," chimed Big Sister, "some of them eat thousands of times their body weight!"

"Holy smokes!" Dad gulped. "I didn't know that. But there's more. Caterpillars are meant to become beautiful butterflies through a process called *metamorphosis*. It's kind of like how we are meant to become wonderful new creatures through Jesus."

"Hey, look what I found!" chirped Little Sister, holding up a tiny ACORN.

Dad stroked his chin, "There's something special about an acorn."

"They're a squirrel's favorite snack!" blurted Little Sister.

"Not mine," Big Brother jumped in, "they're really bitter!"

Dad laughed, "I remember trying those acorns! But there's more. Even though the acorn is small, if it buries roots deep in the ground it will grow into a strong oak that can't be toppled. It's kind of like how if we bury our own roots deep in the teachings of Jesus it will be hard to topple us, too!"

"Aww . . . that's a cute LIZARD!" cooed Big Sister.

"There's something special about a lizard," Dad nodded. "It's *cold-blooded!*" added Big Brother.

"That's right," continued Dad. "The lizard basks in warm places filled with light. It can't live without the sun. We're not so different ourselves. If we'll look for the good in others and spend our time seeking the Light of the World, we'll be happier, too."

The trail curved near the edge of the lake.

Curiously, his sisters gathered to look. Sure enough, three faces stared back at them.

Smiling, Dad crouched low, his *reflection* joining theirs. "There's something really special about each of you."

"We know," giggled Little Sister. "You love us!"

Dad laughed too, squeezing them in a big bear hug.
"That's right, you are my children, and I love you tons!
You are also children of God, and He loves you too!"

Soon, Little Sister's feet started to drag.
"Dad, I'm tired. Can you carry me?"

"I'll carry you," offered Big Sister.

She squeezed Little Sister around the middle and grunted, lifting
her only an inch off the ground. "Ughhh, you're too heavy!"
Dad chuckled, "I'll carry you," and he
hoisted her onto his shoulders.

"Look at the pretty MOON!" exclaimed Big Sister.

"It's gorgeous!" agreed Dad. "And there's something special about it, too."

"I know!" claimed Big Brother,
"It's 239,000 miles from Earth!"

"That's a long way!" Dad said thoughtfully. "But there's more.
The moon actually doesn't make its own light. It only reflects
the sun's light. By doing so, it helps us find our way home.
It's kind of like how we can reflect the light of Jesus to
help others find their way home to Him."

"Hey! I see our STARS," Big Brother pointed.

"They're so twinkly," added Big Sister.
"Aren't they beautiful?" asked Dad.
Little Sister interrupted, "Can we just keep going? I'm tired."
Dad chuckled, "You bet! But first, there's something very
special about the stars."

"They're *billions* of years old!"
shouted Big Sister.
"Wow!" Dad breathed, "That's old!
But there's more. On clear nights like
this, you can look up and see a gazillion
stars. On others, you can't see a thing! It's
kind of like how we sometimes see the hand
of God in our lives. Other times we don't. It
doesn't mean He isn't there, it just means
something is in the way."

"We're almost home! I'll race ya!"
Big Brother challenged.

Big Sister and Big Brother sped off, leaving Dad
and Little Sister trailing behind. Out of breath,
the kids slipped off their shoes and headed
towards the front door.

Little Sister wrapped her little arms around Dad, hugging him tight.

"Dad, there *is* something special about a walk! Thanks for showing us!"

Author

Ryan Marsh is a Tennessee-based author with Alaskan roots. He enjoys inspirational writing for children to encourage higher thinking. He has a BS in Finance from Brigham Young University and works in Nashville for a global fintech company. Given the choice between a mountain camping trip and a stay at the Ritz Carlton, he'd choose camping . . . at *least* half the time.

Illustrator

Kelly Smith is a freelance illustrator based in Atlanta, GA, originally from Peru. She has an MFA in Animation from Savannah College of Art and Design and a BA in illustration from Brigham Young University. She loves to make uplifting illustrations and tell beautiful stories. Follow her on Instagram: @kellysmith.art

To find out more about Ryan's children's book, Something Special,
follow him on Instagram: @ryan.sdmh